MAKANDAL
The Black Messiah
2nd Edition

FRANTZ DERENONCOURT, JR.
Illustrated by Eminence System

Summary: An in-depth account of the life of the maroon leader, Makandal, who fought relentlessly to free Africans from French colonial rule in Haiti.

ISBN – 978-1-7367256-1-0

Stay connected with Thorobred Books at www.thorobredbooks.com

Special Thanks

Thank you to my ancestors for inspiring me to write their memorable stories. Those that have never heard names like; Makandal, Boukman, Toussaint, Dessalines, Cecile Fatimah, Marie-Jeanne, Sanite Belair, and many others may salute their efforts and recognize them as heroes and sheroes.

"*Until The Lion Learns To Write,
Every Story Will Glorify The Hunter*"

- African Proverb

There was once a talented and gifted boy, the son of a village chief in the area known today as Congo, Africa. It was well known in the village that this 12-year-old boy had advanced abilities such as reading and writing in his family language, Arabic.

This was something only a very small number of people in the area knew how to do. The boy was a masterful artist and would spend his days writing, painting, and playing musical instruments.

One day, the boy's village was raided by slave traders. These men would storm into villages in Africa, kidnap millions of people, and sell them as slaves thousands of miles away from their homes.

The boy and his friends had tried to escape the evil men, but it was too late. The boy was captured.

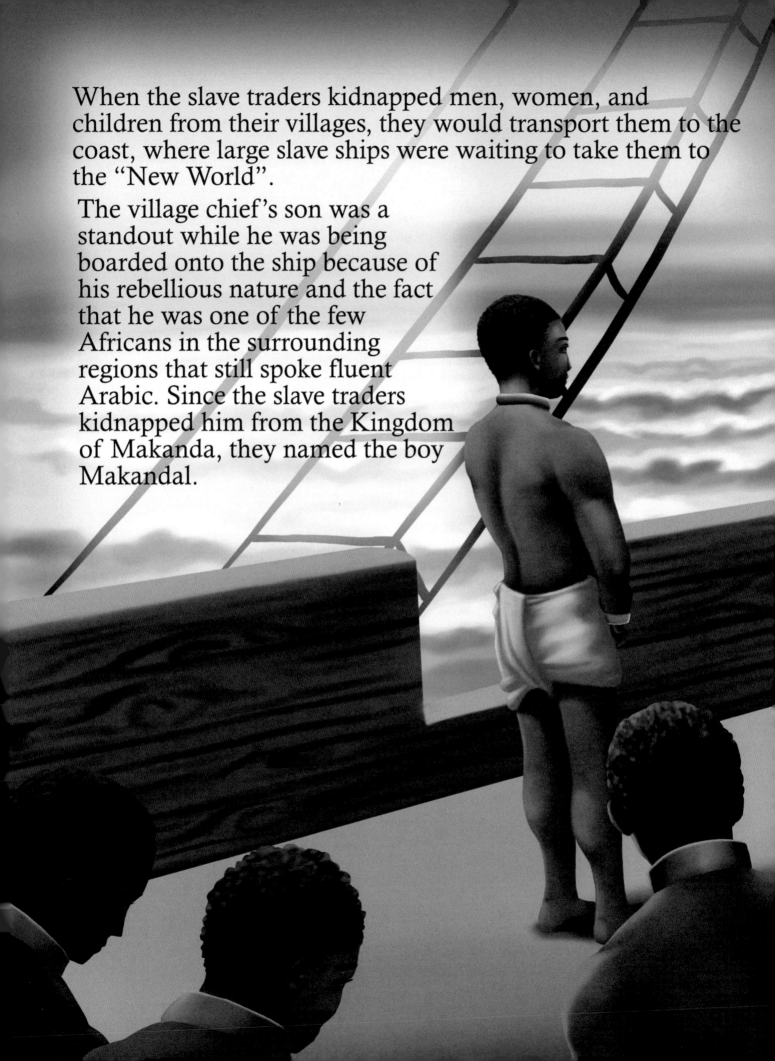

When the slave traders kidnapped men, women, and children from their villages, they would transport them to the coast, where large slave ships were waiting to take them to the "New World".

The village chief's son was a standout while he was being boarded onto the ship because of his rebellious nature and the fact that he was one of the few Africans in the surrounding regions that still spoke fluent Arabic. Since the slave traders kidnapped him from the Kingdom of Makanda, they named the boy Makandal.

The journey to the "New World" was long and scary.
But Makandal remained brave.

Makandal was led off of the slave ship, and he stepped onto land for the first time in over a month. He was told the name of his new home was Saint Domingue, present-day Haiti. Saint Domingue was a colony of France.

Makandal was an instant popular figure on the plantation. The other enslaved people were always in awe of his unique abilities. He was known for his wit and intelligence, and he raised the morale and confidence of all the enslaved Africans around him.

Makandal had become the plantation medicine man because of his vast knowledge of plants. He knew the healing effects of dozens of plants that grew on the island. People from plantations near and far came to him to be cured of different ailments and diseases. He was always happy to help.

On Sundays, when the enslaved Africans were not forced to work on the plantations, Makandal loved telling stories about his ancestors in Africa. People would always gather around to hear him speak.

Makandal had taught himself how to read and speak the French language very quickly and started secretly teaching the other enslaved people on the plantation. Education of the slaves was strictly forbidden in the colony. The slavers started keeping a close eye on him.

Makandal was made to work on the plantation sugar refining factory where millions of pounds of sugar cane were processed for export to France. The factory was a non-stop operation, and enslaved Africans would work there day and night.

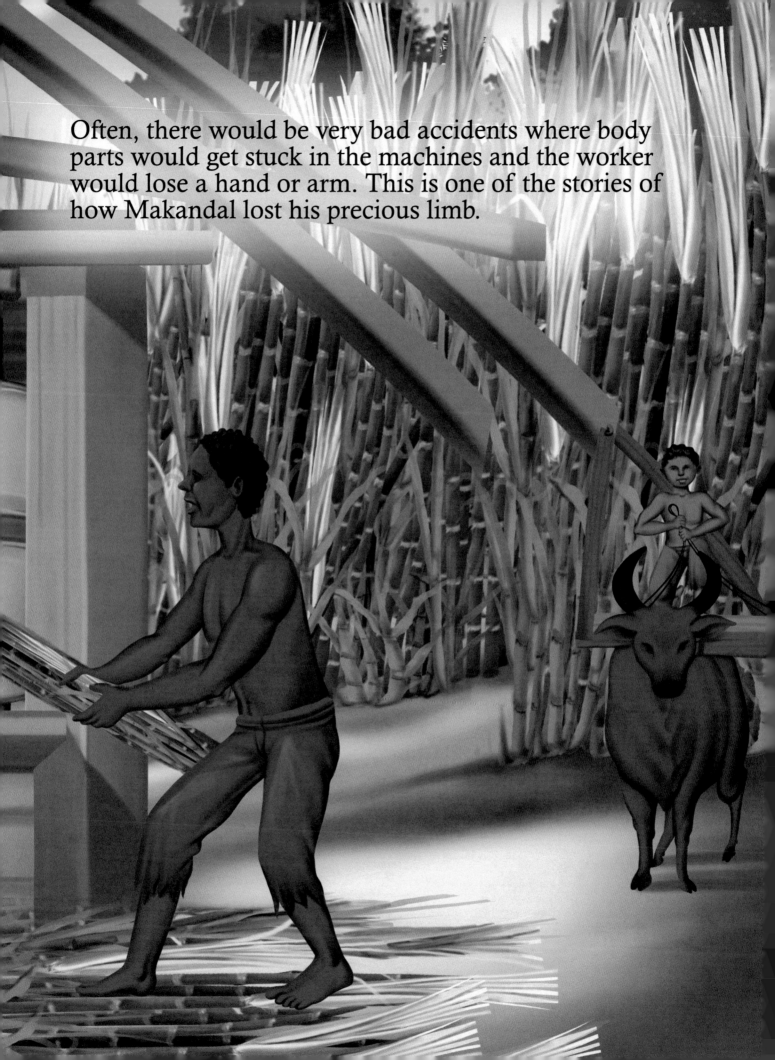

Often, there would be very bad accidents where body parts would get stuck in the machines and the worker would lose a hand or arm. This is one of the stories of how Makandal lost his precious limb.

Now, a young man, Makandal, met an enslaved woman he liked and began to spend time with her. The only problem was that she worked in the slaver's mansion, and he would have to sneak over there to see her. When the slave master saw this, he became very angry and had Makandal captured and sentenced to 50 lashes with a bullwhip, which no person could survive.

While Makandal was receiving his punishment, he managed to break free from his shackles and escape into the mountains.

While in the mountains, Makandal joined a village of maroons. A maroon is a person who had escaped slavery. There were thousands of maroons in the mountains and dozens of maroon villages. While in his village, Makandal began to speak out against the injustice of slavery. He said that slavery was not the reason for their existence. He preached that everyone was equal and deserved to be free, which was the opposite of what the French slavers had told them.

Makandal was able to unite all the different maroon tribes in the mountains with his message, which was to fight for one common goal, an end to the enslavement of their brothers and sisters on the plantation.

Makandal captured the attention of every enslaved person in the colony. Some of them had already accepted their fate as slaves, but Makandal gave them hope.

The maroons would usually band together at night and raid plantations for food, clothes, and other supplies they needed to survive in the mountains. They would also use the raids as an opportunity to recruit new maroons.

Makandal was always one of the most fearless leaders of the maroons, and he was dashing and daring in his conquests. His exploits during the raids would only add to his legend.

During one of the raids, Makandal was caught by the slave drivers and locked up in a jail on the plantation. The penalty for raids against the French slave owners was death. But when the slavers went to Makandal's cell to carry out his sentence, he was gone. He had escaped again.

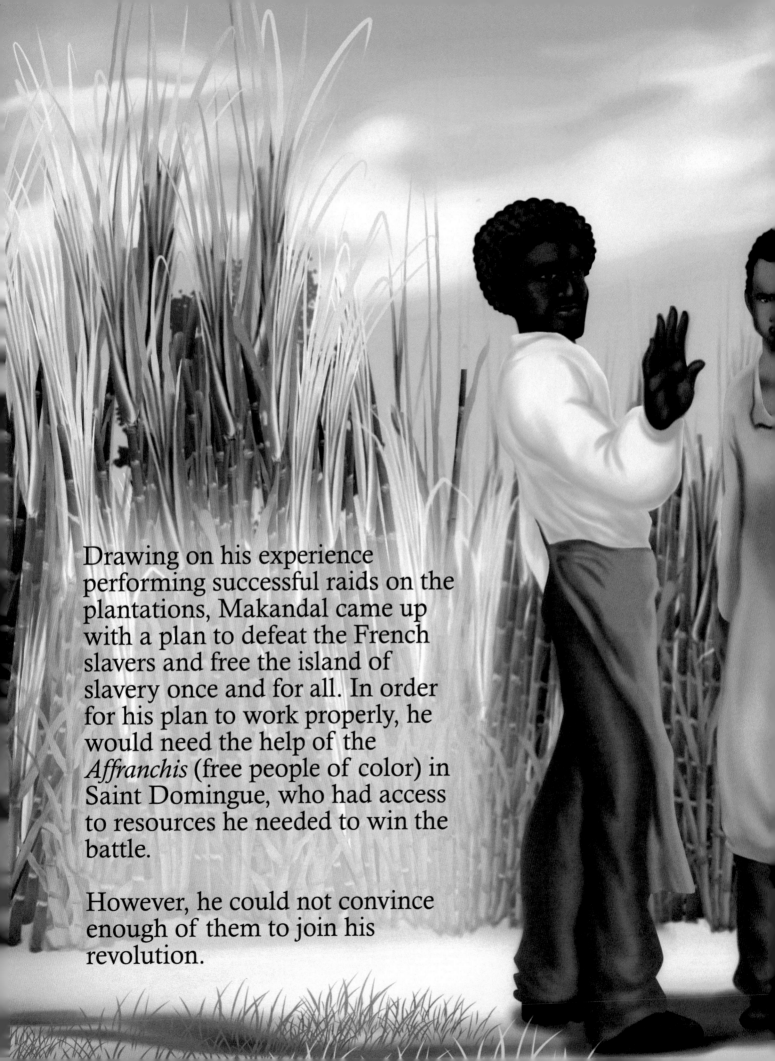

Drawing on his experience performing successful raids on the plantations, Makandal came up with a plan to defeat the French slavers and free the island of slavery once and for all. In order for his plan to work properly, he would need the help of the *Affranchis* (free people of color) in Saint Domingue, who had access to resources he needed to win the battle.

However, he could not convince enough of them to join his revolution.

Even though he did not get much support from the *Affranchis*, Makandal did not give up on his plan to end the enslavement of his people. He decided to fight his enemy using what he knew best, plants. Just as he knew how to create medicine from plants, he also knew how to make poison. He formed a plan to make thousands of portions of poison using the native plants in the mountains and distribute them to his vast network of people on the plantations.

They would put the poison in the slavers' food and drinks. After the slave owners had fallen sick from the poison, he would attack the plantation with his maroon army.

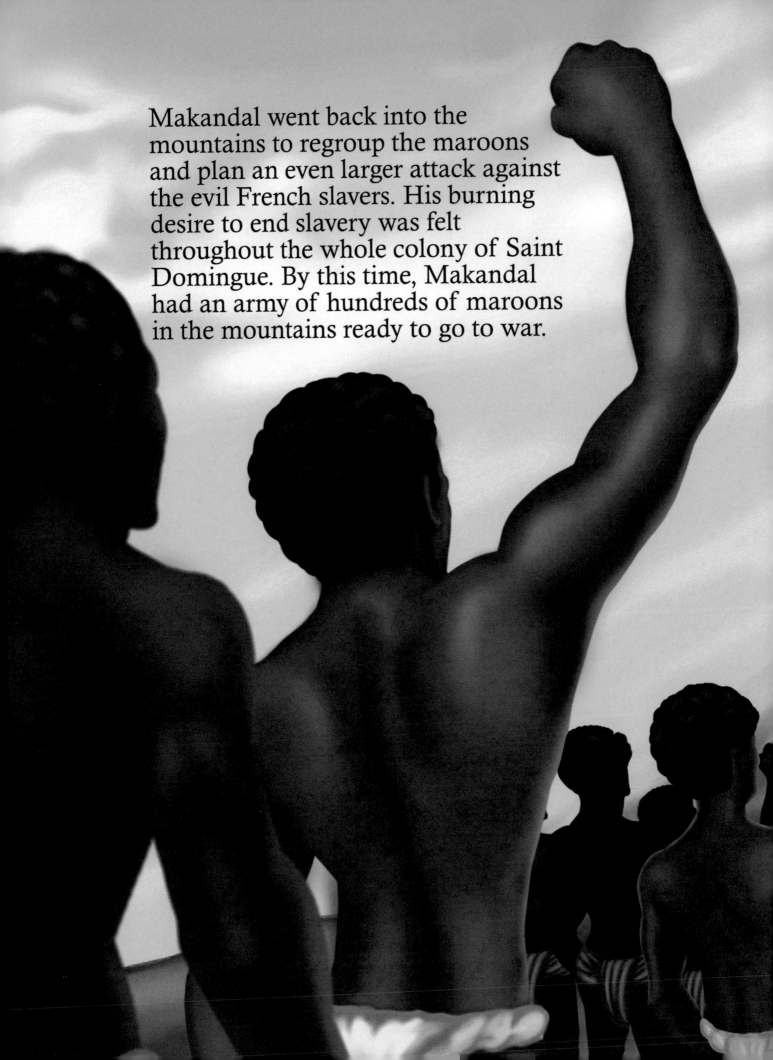

Makandal went back into the mountains to regroup the maroons and plan an even larger attack against the evil French slavers. His burning desire to end slavery was felt throughout the whole colony of Saint Domingue. By this time, Makandal had an army of hundreds of maroons in the mountains ready to go to war.

The French slavers knew Makandal was a big problem and could jeopardize the whole system of slavery, which they depended on for their wealth. They decided to go to extreme measures to try and find him.

The slave drivers would look for people they suspected knew where he was hiding and began to torture them for information. The pain was so unbearable that some of them finally agreed to help set a trap to capture him. The slavers sent their guards to take Makandal into custody.

After many failed attempts, they eventually arrested him.

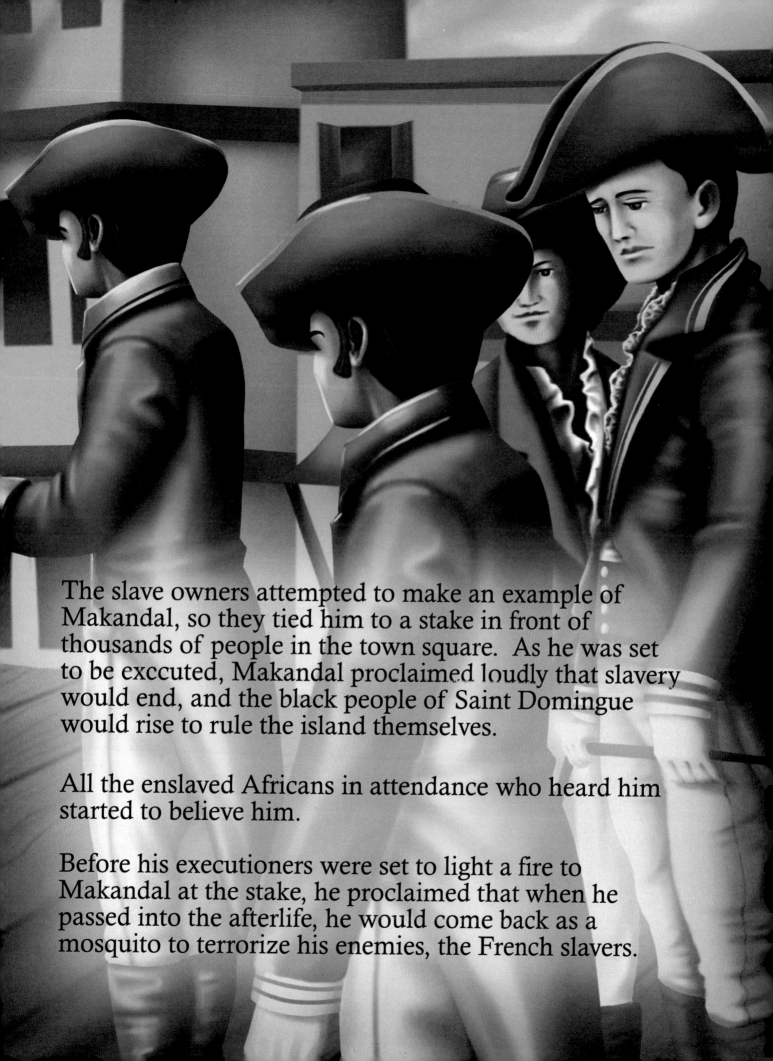

The slave owners attempted to make an example of Makandal, so they tied him to a stake in front of thousands of people in the town square. As he was set to be exccuted, Makandal proclaimed loudly that slavery would end, and the black people of Saint Domingue would rise to rule the island themselves.

All the enslaved Africans in attendance who heard him started to believe him.

Before his executioners were set to light a fire to Makandal at the stake, he proclaimed that when he passed into the afterlife, he would come back as a mosquito to terrorize his enemies, the French slavers.

There are many different versions of what happened that day on January 20, 1758. Some say that he broke free from his bonds and escaped into the mountains, while some say he perished at the stake. Either way, Makandal was never heard from again.

Thirty-three years after Makandal's disappearance, a maroon named Dutty Boukman held a secret ceremony at the same site where Makandal had made some of his inspiring speeches. The site is known as Bwa Kayiman, the birthplace of the Haitian Revolution. Haiti won its independence from France, and on January 1, 1804, became the first free black nation in the western hemisphere.

One of the many reasons that Haitian rebels were victorious in their war for independence was the rapid spread of yellow fever that claimed the lives of over twenty thousand European soldiers. The deadly virus was spread by an infestation of mosquitoes. To this day, many Haitians believe that the infestation of mosquitoes was the reincarnation of the African village chief's son, Makandal.

Also from

Thorobred Books

Get the whole

Haitian Heroes

Collection

at

www.thorobredbooks.com

Made in the USA
Middletown, DE
14 June 2022